Hidden Treasures

A Collection of Godly Inspirations to Bless your Soul

Volume I

Wanda Dawson

Scripture quotations taken from: The Holy New King James Version of the Bible. Copyright 1979, 1980, 1982 by Thomas Nelson, Inc. Used by permission. All rights reserved. Those marked "AMPC" are taken from the Amplified Bible Classic Edition. Copyright 1954, 1958, 1964,1965, 1987 by the Lockman Foundation.. Those marked "OJB" are taken from the Oxford Jewish Bible. Copyright 2002, 2003, 2008, 2010, 2011 by Artists for Israel International, Inc. Used by permission. All rights reserved. Those marked "KJV" are taken from *The Holy Bible, King James Version*. Copyright 1977, 1984, Thomas Nelson Inc., Publishers. Those marked "ESV" are taken from The Holy Bible, English Standard Version. Copyright 2001 by Crossway. All rights reserved. Those marked "NIV" are taken from the Holy Bible, New International Version. Copyright 1973, 1978, 1984 by Biblica, Inc. All rights reserved. Those marked "NAS" are taken from the New American Standard Version. Copyright 1971. Grateful acknowledgement is made to Teresa Skinner for permission to use her song, "Wash Away All", written by Teresa Skinner. Copyright 2005.

© 2018 Wanda Dawson
All rights reserved.
ISBN: 1981159517
ISBN-13: 9781981159512
Library of Congress Control Number: 2017919535
CreateSpace Independent Publishing Platform
North Charleston, South Carolina

I would like to dedicate this book to my grandmother Anna Borzel (our family affectionately called her Gramby). I have always known her as strong, courageous, and thankful. She encouraged us to think positively about the many situations life handed us. I recall days as a child visiting her during summer holidays, when I knew life was hard and trying for my grandmother, yet Gramby was whistling or singing a tune—giving glory to her Heavenly Father. I have learned so much from my dear grandmother. She was such a good example of Jesus and His love, not just by words but by her actions and attitude. She tried to see the best in people.

June 17, 2016, Gramby passed on from this life. I miss her. I know that "we are surrounded by so great a cloud of witnesses" "of which she is one." (Heb. 11:1).

I treasure the years Gramby was with us!

Acknowledgments

I WANT TO thank all those who have shared their "treasures." You have made this book become a reality by giving something of yourself in order to touch and encourage another life.

Contents

Acknowledgments		v
Introduction		ix
Chapter 1	Encouragement and Blessings	1
Chapter 2	Wash Away All	6
Chapter 3	God of the Little Things	9
Chapter 4	God is Faithful	12
Chapter 5	The Lord is My Shepherd	16
Chapter 6	Walking with God	21
Chapter 7	The Blessings of Bible Verses	26
Chapter 8	Belonging	29
Chapter 9	Forgiveness	32
Chapter 10	Answered Prayer	37
Chapter 11	God is So Good	43
Chapter 12	Jesus Christ, My Redeemer	46
Chapter 13	The Power of Blessing and Our Words	51
About the Author		53

Introduction

I WOULD LIKE to explain what I mean by "treasures". For me a *treasure*, is a very precious package given by someone else to me. When a person shares with me something that God has done in their life, they are giving me a part of themselves. The person may or may not have any idea that they are blessing me. God knows exactly what I have need of every day and I believe that He specifically and strategically places people in my path, to touch and minister to me.

I used to be very shy, in my growing up years and into my adult years. People would stand up in church and give a testimony. I know that they were sharing about how their Heavenly Father had touched or blessed them; but to me they appeared very brave to do this. And so I understand those that have a difficult time sharing or witnessing.

God put on my heart to put this book together, as well as additional volumes in the future. He had "shy and quiet" people in mind, to enable them and give them a platform to voice their *treasures*. I have collected many of these *treasures* to share with you. They have come from many nations--Canada, United States, Africa, and other places. I pray that you are blessed, encouraged, and ministered to as your read the pages before you.

Chapter 1

Encouragement and Blessings

The verses of 1 Corinthians 12 speak about gifts of, and within, the body of Christ. There are diversities of gifts and specific gifts. It is so amazing to me how God *gifts* us with our gift(s).

As a child I took great delight in serving and loving others, and this has continued to this present day. When I was twelve, God impressed on me that I would go to Africa to be a missionary. Many, many years have gone by since that day and I have not gone to Africa, but God always connects me with people from Africa. I have always loved these dear people. I know God put this in me.

Heavenly Father intrigues me. He has given me prophetic art. I say this because I really cannot draw. Since a child, I have had pictures in my head—but stick figure drawings are all that would come out on the paper. He gives me visions and pictures, then takes my inabilities and anoints my fingers and I produce amazing pictures with pastels! I praise God for these gifts that He has given me. It shows me how awesome He is and how He is not limited to my humanness, as I am. He can do whatever He wants with this piece of clay.

WANDA DAWSON
Edmonton, Alberta

Gramby is a young married woman with two toddlers at her side. It is her job to bring in the firewood to cook and warm the house with. Well, here is this log. And here is her saw. It is a two-man crosscut saw. (It takes two people to operate this kind of saw—one person pulls toward him- or herself, and then the person on the other end pulls toward him- or herself—get the picture?) Anyway, here is this young woman outside with the saw, the log, and two toddlers. Gramby places the saw on the log and pulls—now, who is going to pull back? Gramby pushes this bendable saw out—very difficult! Then she pulls to herself and then p-u-s-h-e-s it back. Struggle. Struggle. She is crying and probably praying. All of a sudden *someone* pulls the saw, Gramby pulls, *someone* pulls, and Gramby pulls. *Someone* pulls. Gramby gets the log sawed. Thank you, *someone*. God does care about these things. (Written by Gramby's oldest child, my mother.)

KAROL
Prince George, British Columbia

When my little baby girl was born, I got to watch my husband become a father. I got to witness the miracle of birth and life on his face, and what I saw I will never forget. I saw wonder, awe, unconditional love, joy, and perhaps a touch of fear of the unknown. Now as I watch the two of them together, I get to revisit that day as those same emotions light up his face. I am in complete awe of my husband as he gently holds our little girl, as he brings a smile to her face, as he helps her to walk and eat, as he dreams of what the future is going to hold for her, as he prays for her. I get to watch my husband become a father every day. What an honor! What a privilege!

JANNELL
Edmonton, Alberta

Having five kids is challenging enough—what's more, being a single mom with five kids plus a dog! This is my life. But God has been great to me all the time! That's why, as for me and my house, we will serve the Lord all the time.

With five kids, calling a family meeting is easy. I turn off the Wi-Fi router and wait where the Wi-Fi is located. Also, I swear I have two mysterious people living in my house: Somebody and Nobody. Somebody did it, and Nobody knows who.

It's a blessing to have five kids and a dog! I love it! You just have to remain faithful and be on your knees every day. It's true—God will supply all your needs! Thank you, Lord.

ROCHELIE
Philippines/Edmonton, Alberta

The doorbell rang. On the porch stood three members of our church carrying boxes, which they brought into the house while explaining that someone had brought the boxes to the church too late to be included in the Christmas hampers. They took the matter to the Lord, asking who needed the supplies. When our name came to mind, they all agreed. They were bringing the boxes of food to us. The next day three extended family members arrived unannounced to spend the holidays with us. They were concerned with how we could feed them, so we took them downstairs and showed them the boxes of food that the Lord had provided for us and them. The boxes of food lasted until the day our guests left. What a marvelous holiday! What a great God!

KEN and MYRNA
Prince George, British Columbia

My husband had gone for his driver's test many times and did not pass. He really needed to have his license. A lady at the church he was preaching at asked if he had a car. Apparently, my husband had mentioned something about a car in one of his Sunday messages. This lady wanted to give us her deceased husband's car. This was in May.

My husband went again in July, took his driver's test, and got it within a very short time. Very soon after this success, we were contemplating renting a vehicle to just go for a drive. Once we found out the price, we decided that it would make more sense to put the money toward car insurance. We arrived at the insurance place as the last customers; they even had their Closed sign up. That same day, we contacted the lady with the car to see if it worked for her if we came by. She was pleased to give us her husband's car and being that it was the anniversary of his death, we could sense that she was content with giving it to us. She asked if we would mind if she anointed the car. We were OK with it.

Then she asked if we minded if she pray in tongues. We were surprised but pleased by these things because we had no idea that she did them—the church she attended did not demonstrate these.

We are very thankful to have a nice, God-given car to drive. Who knows—maybe one day I will go and get my license.

CLARA
Zimbabwe, Africa/Edmonton, Alberta

My mom is my treasure.

Why is my mom my hidden treasure? When I was very sick—and I mean very, very sick—my mom showed me nothing but absolute support. She was never worried for my life because of her trust and faith in Jesus. I was an awful and very angry patient from what I remember. I closed myself off from the world. My friends were worried about me, wondering why I wasn't keeping in contact with them. They found it unusual for my character. I wasn't convinced that my treatment would work because I've known of so many that don't win the battle.

My mom never let me think I wouldn't see the other side. I was so terrified for my life because I felt I was no longer in control of it. I was so weak from my treatment and was in for a long journey to overcome this deadly disease. After my first session of treatment, I fell very ill with a fever and had to get treated at the hospital. My mom came every day to the hospital to visit me and would have dinner with me. We would go for a walk, and I wheeled my IV stand.

When I got to leave the hospital later in the week, I was back to my old hermit-like self. My mom didn't want me to be this way. She said she hadn't seen me smile in months. My mom had me go for daily walks with her and the dog, rain or shine—even if I didn't want to go, she insisted. She didn't want me to get into a darker and darker place. She would hold my hand as we walked and chatted. I could feel her love and strength, and I felt truly safe. She strongly encouraged me to reach out to my worried friends to let them know what was going on with me. After a little while, I did reach out to my close friends, and initially they were angry at me—angry because I didn't tell them what was going on with me. I went out for coffee with a few of my closest friends, and it was the beginning of me feeling alive again and somewhat normal.

I had so much support from my friends and family the moment I let them in to support me through this journey. I am one of the lucky ones to make it to the other side and live a full and normal life. I witnessed my mom's undying faith in Jesus that gave her the strength to help me through probably the darkest time in my life. My mom is truly the most selfless person I know, and that is why she is my treasure.

JENNY
Edmonton, Alberta

CHAPTER 2

Wash Away All

Wash away all my bitterness,
My selfishness, my loneliness.
Wash away all my bitterness,
My selfishness, my loneliness.

For the world is turning faster,
And soon time will be no more.
How can I reach beyond my walls?

There are so many lonely people,
Many children without care.
Maybe I can give my heart somewhere?

Wash away all my bitterness,
My selfishness, my loneliness.
Wash away all my bitterness,
My selfishness, my loneliness.

Jesus, Jesus…wash away all.

TERESA SKINNER
Prescott, Arizona

The evening my husband left was one of the hardest days yet the biggest relief I have ever felt.

You see, I had been living a lie for more than twelve years. Yes, as a Christian woman, I was making bad choices and breaking the vows I took in front of God and family. You see, I had been hiding my feelings from my husband for so long for fear that I would be rejected and misunderstood. All I wanted was to be understood and heard and safe. This was not possible with him, and although I reached out more times than I remember, I turned to other ways to cope. I binge drank with close friends, and I had numerous affairs. I acted like all was happy and went to church every Sunday, but I hid what was really in my heart. My close friends knew the struggle; I couldn't tell anyone else. I was ashamed of who I was, what I had done, and what I was doing. I felt worthless and suicidal, dealing with depression and anxiety throughout my marriage, yet I was happy with so many things in my life—especially my three wonderful boys.

Fast forward to after my separation; I never wanted to live so bad to prove that I could be a good mother and be alive and do right by my boys—raise them how I knew I could and be a good role model and mother. I had no idea my husband would use every means possible to ruin every relationship I had—including those with our boys. He went to great lengths to expose my affairs, my misspending, my messy house, and any other shred of evidence to get my family, my church, and my friends to turn against me. He hacked e-mails and my computer and did everything possible to prove I was unfit. I would cry out to God to stop him. Stop the pain and stop the hurt I had so deep in my heart. One thing that I always thought was, I am not going to fight dirty. It was not right to fight back with evil. I would hold my head up and try and do right. For once in my life I would do something right.

I had read so many books about divorce and parenting. All I really needed was the Bible and then to have help interpreting it for me—a child of God. I found some helpful books to help me understand God's love for me and His grace. See, the hardest thing was forgiving myself. I still struggle to do this; however, every day I get stronger and let God's love surround me increasingly. I kept people from getting close because I didn't think people would love me if they knew the real me. Well, God loves me unconditionally. Nothing I do will make Him love me less, and nothing I have done in my past will make Him love me less or more. I don't know what I would have done without this love. God has sent me people to love me, help heal me, and guide me to Him—even though I feel sometimes that I was punished by God in my dealings with judges and court and people. I know God had His hand in it—to teach me some hard lessons and to help build me to be the stronger woman I am today. I am proud to say I did what I felt what was best for my kids at the time, and I didn't fight dirty. If I do anything right in this life, I hope that one of them will be that I tried my best to honor God in my divorce proceedings. God paved the way for me, and I will be faithful and trust Him in all situations. I trusted Him with my divorce, and He became more real than He ever had been in all my life. Praise be to God for His love and faithfulness.

ANONYMOUS
Edmonton, Alberta

CHAPTER 3

God of the Little Things

MY HEART IS warmed as I remember the many ways that God has shown me that He cares for me in the little things.

For instance, years back, when I still used hair spray to keep my curls in place (artificial curls from a perm), I had bought a brand-new can of hair spray. The first time I tried to use it, it went "sspizzile, sspet." I tried it again—and again. I took the little spout off, rinsed it well, and replaced it on the can but no spray—just this fizzly noise. I took it apart again, washed it, rinsed it, checked for any obstruction—nothing. I put the spout back on, looked at the can, and said, "Lord, it sure would be nice if this thing worked," *and it did!* For the rest of the can, I had a constant, steady spray—right to the last drop.

Does God care about the little things? Oh yes, He does. Praises go to my God for caring.

My husband, Tom, was out on one of his many adventures. One day he was out in the bush with his little pickup. He had his power saw, his ax, and his big muscles. Once he had the pickup full of blocks of wood, he saw that it was time to get home, unload the pickup, and head off to his afternoon shift at the pulp mill. But his pickup was stuck, like, really deep. So he put branches under the tires (which spun uselessly in the mud) and tried again and again and again. No success—the tires went deeper and deeper into the mud. Time was passing, and he had to get to work. So he prayed, got into the pickup, and drove right out. Who pushed?

※

A cow had given birth. She then got some kind of infection and was going downhill fast. Not eating or drinking. Tom sat on a hay bale and talked to God. He said, "God, a cow can't live if she doesn't drink." He asked the Lord to get the cow to drink. The cow staggered over to the water trough and drank. Next day, Tom sat on the hay bale and talked to God: "God, a cow can't live if she doesn't eat." The cow went at the hay bale. That cow lived for many more years, producing a calf every year. By the way, all the time that mama cow was not eating and drinking, her baby kept sucking. Don't know what nourishment she was getting, but the calf survived as well.

KAROL
Prince George, British Columbia

※

I was driving home from my bible study group's Christmas party and had most likely not been paying attention to my surroundings. (That is what too much food and fun do to you).

As I made a right turn to go into our neighborhood, I noticed a police vehicle with its lights flashing behind me. There wasn't anybody else on the road in the same direction that I was heading, so I figured it has got to be *me*. I signaled to the right and pulled over.

The usual drill—I was asked for my drivers license and vehicle registration. After handing them over, the officer asked if I knew what he had stopped me for? I told him that I had an idea of what it might be and it was my outstanding speeding tickets that I found in my purse recently (that I had forgotten to attend to, but was something that I was going to attend to in the upcoming week). The officer tells me that the unpaid tickets were not the reason, but the fact that I did not stop at the red light before making a right turn into the neighborhood. I apologized profusely and told him that it had been a long day, and that I honestly did not remember noticing the red light.

He and the other officer proceeded to head back to their vehicle. At that very moment, I asked God for His grace and how badly I needed it then. I prayed that He would somehow get me out of the bind by speaking to the officer's hearts and give me grace to redeem myself. Numbers started going through my head as I crazily did the math of how much the "damages" would be including my existing, outstanding photo radar tickets! I approximated the amount to be around eight hundred dollars. And with that alone, I found myself again praying, desperately begging God for His mercy and grace!

When the officer came back, after running a check on my license, it turns out that I have another, much more grave offence. And that is a nine month expired registration! (Remember how we no longer get a reminder in the mail for this?!)

But God's grace prevailed. The officer told me how my offences this evening alone, is a penalty of at least six hundred dollars. But since he has run out of tickets, he could not write me one and he is letting me off the hook!

And yes indeed, I will be taking care of my registration and unpaid radar tickets first thing tomorrow morning!

Thank you Father God for your mercy and grace, in so many different ways. Indeed, they are too great to comprehend. What a blessing, a very early and much appreciated present for Christmas!

SHARON
Manila, Philippines/Edmonton, Alberta

CHAPTER 4

God is Faithful

A TESTIMONY OF God's provision while in Bible school: The day came when we had only some macaroni noodles and some oatmeal in the cupboard. Henry felt maybe God wouldn't mind if we used some of our tithe to buy groceries. I reminded him that scripture said we were to give all our tithes. We took our tithes to the church on our way out of the city. When we got home, there was a message from the church. They had had a grocery shower for us, and we needed to go and get it. There were enough groceries to feed us for three months. Our God is faithful!

HENRY AND JANET
Winfield, Alberta

In 1975, my work's head office asked me to move to Prince George. I was not sure if this was God's will. The scriptures tell us that the Lord orders the steps of a righteous man. It was a Wednesday, and I was driving home from work, and God told me we were to move to Prince George. The presence of the Lord was very strong in the vehicle. I drove home crying my eyes out. I knew beyond any doubt that we were to move. I knew—oh how I knew. I got home and told my wife, Reta, that we were to move. I called the head office to tell them that I had changed my mind and would go, but was told that the job had been offered to somebody else and that I was to not worry about it. That Friday I received a call from my British Columbia regional manager asking if I was serious. I said yes, and we were on the plane flying to Prince George on Saturday morning. We put an offer on a house, and our house sold a week later, even though everyone told us we would not get the price we were asking. We received an offer and a backup offer. This goes to show you that if it is God's plan for you, He will bring it to pass. We moved to Williams Lake in 1984 to take over the company branch there.

Reta took sick with cancer in 1996. That was the last year we had Christmas together. We had our struggles with finances, and so money was tight. The day Reta was seen by a doctor in an emergency, they made an appointment for us to be in Prince George for further testing. We needed new snow tires for the car, as this was in November, and I said we didn't have the money, but Reta said, "I don't care; go and buy them anyway." The Lord had put it in Reta's heart to buy them. Unbeknownst to us, Monday morning, as we were leaving Williams Lake for Prince George, a Greyhound bus had gone off the road, and the police were having trouble standing on the road because it was pure ice. Thank the Lord that we had new studded snow tires, and we could travel to Prince George safely. Reta passed away September 17, 1997—twelve days before her fifty-third birthday. The Lord gave me such peace at her passing. The Bible tells us that Jesus will give us a peace that passes all understanding, and truly that is what I experienced.

I met my present wife online—something I said I would never do. I agreed to go on Christian Mingle just to shut my friends and daughter-in-law up. The Lord again directed my path. Doreen and I met for coffee when I had to go to Kelowna for medical reasons, and our coffee and lunch date lasted five hours. I never expected anything to come of it, but the Lord had other plans. I told Doreen that I was not moving, because I fished and hunted, and all my friends were in Williams Lake. She said that she would move, as her place was only a house. On the way home, I felt the Lord's presence in the car, and He said to me, "Gary, she is willing to move—what about you?"

Again, I cried my eyes out as I drove home, knowing that God wanted me to move. Over the next five months, we were in daily contact on the computer and two to three hours on the phone. The Lord gave Doreen a scripture that says, "For I know the plans I have for you," declares the Lord, "plans to prosper you and not to harm you, plans to give you hope and a future." (Jeremiah 29:11, NIV). She has this on a plaque. In our four years of marriage, God has blessed both of us beyond measure. I am so thankful to the Lord for His leading and guiding all through my life. Yes, I have made mistakes, and some have been bad and had consequences, but God is faithful if we fully trust in Him. David says in the Psalms that His Word is a light and guide to my path.

GARY
Kelowna, British Columbia

The Lord really showed Himself true and faithful one sunny August afternoon in 2011. I was traveling alone on my way from Prince George to Dawson Creek for a surprise birthday party when at a highway construction stop, my car would not start when it was time for the lineup to leave. Instant fear and panic started to infiltrate my mind. I cried out aloud, "No, Lord, no. This can't be happening. Lord, I need you!" I felt so vulnerable. Most women hate when something mechanical goes wrong in their car. As a paraplegic, I was at a greater disadvantage than most. There I was, stuck in the middle of the beautiful mountains with burly men and no cell service. Imagine my discomfort, fear, and panic.

As I sat there, trying to start my car, the flag person came over and asked in his gruff voice, "What's wrong?" I could see he was a bit impatient. I tried to explain to him that my car wouldn't start and that I was in a wheelchair and therefore couldn't be of much assistance. Upon hearing that information, he immediately called for their heavy-duty mechanic to see if he could come and figure out the problem. Two mechanics came, and after trying to decipher what the issue was and coming up with no solution, they decided to push my car to the only spot on the opposite side of the road. It was sheer cliff but with just enough clearing for my car! Knowing my car was not drivable, we now had to figure out what to do with me. I couldn't be left on the side of a mountain, and there was no cell service to call my sister for help. So they decided to have a crew member drive me in one of their vehicles to the little café where they all camped at. Sounds great, right? Well, when the person arrived, he had the biggest work truck I had ever seen! I was thinking, How on earth am I going to get into that truck? No sooner had the thought crossed my mind and panic set in then I felt a tap on the shoulder and the words, "Hey, Cuz, whatcha doin'?"

I whipped my head around, and there was my cousin James, who I had not seen in few years. I was so shocked and surprised he was there; it felt surreal. I was stumbling over my words, I said, "What? What are you doing here?"

He replied, "My buddies and I got called in for a job. We are on the way to work at a camp in Chetwynd. I was sleeping in the back when we had to stop for the construction, and when I woke up, I saw you getting out of your car."

I was so relieved and in shock at the same time. I explained what I needed, the three of them boosted me into the worker's truck, and away we went to the café with them following so they could lift me out of the truck and back into my wheelchair. It was a fifteen- to twenty-minute drive.

God is so good. He knows what is going to happen before we do, and He always looks after the minor details.

What were the chances that my cousin just happened to be going to work that day on that specific highway and just happened to wake up at that construction site and just happened to see me getting out of my car? Remember he hadn't seen me in years, and for him to recognize me was amazing too, as I live in Vancouver.

To add to God's glory, the owner of the cafe had her sister visiting that day, and she was a nurse—not just any nurse but one who worked with spinal cord injuries. Coincidence? I don't think so. Also, I love children, and the owner's grandchildren happened to be visiting her that day, and they were the sweetest, most adorable, and most mature boy and girl. They kept me entertained all day long till my sister and her husband could pick me up.

This experience was a huge faith builder for me. I often look back on it and smile, knowing God has me covered no matter what situation. For those of you who are wondering what was wrong with my car—it was the timing chain.

SHERRIE
Vancouver, British Columbia

CHAPTER 5

The Lord is My Shepherd

MY DAD WAS a mute as my mom used to call him, because every time we asked him a question, he either ignored us or simply replied with an "umm" (meaning yes) or a big "no." My dad watched my sister get baptized in our church. Two years later, he also attended my brother's baptismal service in the same church. Every time Pastor S. visited him at home, he politely turned Pastor S. away. He became very ill when he was ninety-one and was admitted to General Hospital long-term care—so very ill that he could die any second. Every day I tried to convince him to accept Christ, but I didn't know how to start this difficult conversation about his death.

One day I decided to use Psalm 23 to talk about death with him:

> The Lord is my shepherd; I shall not want. He makes me to lie down in green pastures: He leads me beside the still waters. He restores my soul; He leads me in the paths of righteousness For His name's sake. Yea, though I walk through the valley of the shadow of death, I will fear no evil: for You are with me; Your rod and Your staff they comfort me. You prepare a table before me in the presence of my enemies; You anoint my head with oil; My cup runs over. Surely goodness and mercy shall follow me all the days of my life: and I will dwell in the house of the Lord forever. (Psalm 23:1–6, NKJV)

After reading Psalm 23 to him, I asked him, "Dad, would you rather be walking the valley of the shadow of death alone or having Jesus walk with you and without fear?"

He said, "I already believe in Jesus Christ."

I asked him how, and he said Pastor Wong came to his room every second day and led him to Jesus. I called on Pastor Wong to meet me in Dad's hospital room. I asked Pastor Wong to lead my dad into the sinner's prayer. He said he already had, but I insisted on hearing it myself. When Pastor Wong was leading the sinner's prayer, my dad followed him word for word 100 percent. I had never heard my dad speak more than two sentences in one sitting—wow!

The day after my dad was baptized, he sang "Psalm 100" and "Amazing Grace" with us so beautifully that I had no idea where that voice was coming from. I looked at Pastor S., my son, and Brother Greg. It wasn't coming from any of them but from my dad. He might have been a mute but not "tune dead." I was almost in tears because my mom was married to my dad for twenty-five years, and she died without ever hearing my dad hum a single tune. She had called my dad a mute since I was very young.

After my dad was baptized, he fully recovered. We visited him every week to sing with him and brought him communion once a month. Later, he asked for a study Bible, and I gave him a simplified version from Old Testament to New Testament. He read about how Jesus was born, died, and resurrected and the meaning of His death. Those were the most wonderful two years of his life and mine as well. He died peacefully at the age of ninety-three on December 31, 2007.

I want to thank my Father in heaven for giving me the best two years with my earthly father.

CHERRY
Edmonton, Alberta

"He who dwells in the secret place of the Most High shall abide under the shadow of the Almighty". (Psalm 91:1 NKJV)

"No evil shall befall you, Nor shall any plague come near your dwelling". (Psalm 91:10 NKJV)

ALETHA
Namibia, Africa/Edmonton, Alberta

There was a time when I was irresponsible with my business. Prior to this, the business was going great. It was very busy, and the money was flowing through my fingers like crazy. I was finally getting the salary I wanted for a long time. We hit the downturn of 2008, which affected me in 2009. The decals on my first work van were cracking and peeling. I had in my mind to take the decals off and put new decals on. I had this nagging feeling of "don't do it." I didn't listen. I took them off and never had a chance to put them back on. I lost a lot of business just because people thought I was closed. On top of the slowdown, I probably lost 30 percent of my business. It took months, and it started to really hurt. I started to notice it. I was wondering what to do; I borrowed money to pay the bills and to keep the salary where it had been. I got myself deep in debt. The thought of closing the business came to me, but I would have been worse off if I had. Things started to pick up somewhat. I had a feeling to park the van in the driveway instead of on the street. But I didn't pay attention to that thought. A hollow metal bang in the middle of the night woke me up for a few seconds, but I went back to sleep. Later, I woke up to banging on the door. The police were asking me to come out—someone had totaled my van. Now I must get another van. Through all this time and other happenings, I was complaining to God, and He asked me, "Where is your trust? Are you trusting in yourself or in Me?"

I said, "OK, God, You are on. I cannot make the phone ring or convince people to call me. Only You can do that. I will do the work." Out of nowhere, He landed me some work. One job pulled me out of debt entirely.

ANONYMOUS
Grande Prairie, Alberta

There have been many intervals in my life where I have had to rely solely on God for comfort and support. One of the more traumatic times I have had to endure occurred back in 2015, when my husband underwent a liver transplant. Before he was taken into surgery, Bill declared in faith, "Honey, if I see you after surgery, great. If I die, great. Either way, I am in loving hands."

He made it through surgery, but there were several times when we were unsure whether he was going to survive the ordeal or not. While I waited with our family and friends for Bill to regain consciousness, I often rolled his last words over and over in my mind. Whenever I did this, I was reminded to thank the Creator of the Universe for His comfort and protection. For almost two weeks following the surgery, Bill remained unconscious. Then, just when we thought he was beginning to improve, he had a significant setback that plunged him back into a coma for several days. It was during that time the Holy Spirit reminded me that the Father has given Jesus control of our lives. Every believer's future, not just my husband's, were—and are—in His hands, and nothing can remove us from His loving grip. Jesus affirmed this in John 10:27–29: "My sheep hear my voice, and I know them, and they follow me. I give them eternal life, and they will never perish, and no one will snatch them out of my hand. My Father, who has given them to me, is greater than all, and no one is able to snatch them out of the Father's hand. I and the Father are one" (ESV). It was upon His declaration that both my husband and I staked our claim, and even through that very difficult time, we could fully surrender everything to Him and trust that He knew what was best for us.

Who better was there to care for Bill than the one who gave him life? In fact, I was granted such peace through the Holy Spirit during those dark days that others around me in the ICU and burn unit could draw comfort as I worshipped the God of our Salvation through music. Many songs ministered to those around me, but the song that resonated in my heart during that time was "I Surrender All." To this day, I thank God for the opportunity He gave us; He was (and continues to be) closer to us than a brother. Praise God, through whom all blessings flow!

ROSANNA
Calgary, Alberta

CHAPTER 6

Walking with God

Highlights of my walk with God:

Fifteen years old—the freedom I had to sing at the top of my voice (songs to the Lord) while hanging clothes on the line. I had just been born again, and my soul was alive and filled with joy.
Seventeen years old—marrying a good, solid (God-picked) husband.
Seventeen years old—the night God baptized me in His Holy Spirit. Never did I see such a beautiful night sky as I walked home.
Eighteen and twenty years old—being pregnant. The lives of babies growing within—the product of the love of a husband and wife.
Birthing a baby boy and then a baby girl.
Such treasures from God.
Such responsibility! Raising these two children in the Lord.
Answers to prayer.
Twenty-two years old—having been voted in as Sunday school superintendent and president of the ladies group—scary!
Walking the floor in agony—so scared to take on these responsibilities—me—a girl from the sticks!
God speaking into my heart—my peace I give unto you, as I looked out at a full moon.
Praying for my backslidden dad—it took many years for that prayer to be answered, but it was answered.
I now have a perfect Father in heaven.

Fifty-four years old, after being widowed—experiencing my loving Lord's constant presence and help, working through the many tasks that face a woman on her own.

Experiencing the Lord's love when faced with rejection of loved ones.

And daily—He is with me—my Jesus—constant friend.

KAROL
Prince George, British Columbia

We worry because we want our own way. If our lives were completely surrendered, we wouldn't want our own plans but only to fulfill God's.

We must practice this surrendered life, waiting patiently in our days of uncertainty and difficulty so that He can bring us out into a wealthy place of freedom from our own works. "Rest in the LORD and wait patiently for Him…" (Psalm 37:7, NAS). This is suffering in our flesh, and it's mandatory for a life lived in Christ.

AMBER
Los Angeles, California

As we grow older in life, we experience many things. We observe and ask questions. We try to find answers in the meaning and purpose of life.

As little children, we are taught to follow and obey our parents, elders, and teachers—to obey authorities, keep out of trouble, pray to God, and love one another.

As we become more mature, we ask more questions. Life is more complicated than simple. What is the real meaning of life? What is our life cycle? Be born, go to school, get a job, have a family, grow old, and then die? Is there more to life?

I have come across the saying "Nothing in our life is an accident and things happen for a reason." I firmly believe that. If I would reflect on all the things that happened to me, I would realize that all my failures and successes in life are all interrelated. It is taking one step up at a time. Our failures make us strong. They remind us that we are weak, and God is strong. We shouldn't be so proud of ourselves. We should be more reliant on Him. Our failures remind us that God uses people to teach us lessons in our lives. How to choose better decisions. Our faith and our belief in God give us hope. Without hope, our lives will be meaningless.

One of my favorite verses is, "I can do all things through Christ who strengthens me" (Philippians 4:13, NKJV). It is one of the verses I memorized when I was a teenager. Whenever I say this verse, I feel like I am a super being. I feel like Wonder Woman. It gives me so much energy that lasts more than a day to get me going with my life. I am sure everyone has a favorite song. One of my favorites is "God Will Make a Way." There are times when our problems seem so hard and impossible to solve. We forget that God is powerful—so powerful that He can make the impossible possible.

There are times when I have given up and accepted defeat but turn around and find that God has solved my problems for me. How? I don't know. All I know is that God tells us that He made everything beautiful in His time. We just need to learn to be patient and wait. God always answers our prayers—we just have to listen and distinguish whether He is saying yes, no, or wait.

In this troubled world, there are so many things we don't understand. God is the only one who can give us peace of mind. Like a song, we pray to God that He will give us oil in our lamp to keep us burning until the end of day. Many predict that God is coming soon and all things we see around us (wars, diseases, global warming) are signs that the world is coming to self-destruction. I hope that God brings you peace, hope, and love and that He finds you faithful and your lamp burning until the end.

ANONYMOUS
Edmonton, Alberta

My spiritual journey has been lifted higher every day without me realizing it! Place your eyes on the Lord! He's got it all under control. It all started with no faith at all, and sometimes you must experience to believe in certain things in life! Before I start with my beautiful journey in Christ, I would like to thank the Holy Spirit, who is the guarantee to heaven. Without the Holy Spirit, nothing is possible in the spiritual realms.

My life is a wonderful testimony. I don't complain anymore every time I encounter a problem or hardship or feel lost in life. I always remember this scripture: "Greater is He that's in me than He that is in the world" (1 John 4:4 KJV). Whenever you're feeling down in life or losing hope, my prayer for you is that don't give up. You keep on going, hallelujah! He delivered me from demonic attacks, and so will He deliver you too. All it takes is a hungry, open heart that's full of faith in Jesus. Trust in God; He is in you!

I always declare my mornings. I do this by saying, Lord bless the works of my hands. Let my name be associated with good things. Shield me from persecution and false accusations; guard me against greed, discouragement, and sabotage. I welcome opportunities to grow and mature. Let my actions be in sync with Your will. In Jesus' name, amen. I also watch either the supernatural live show every morning or worshipping one or two of my favorite gospel songs. Then I would pray for a few minutes before I start my day. If possible, always pray in tongues. God will fight every trial over your life—just give it all unto Him. Trust and have faith that it's done in His glorious name. Rebuke the spirit of fear to let go and seek His face. Refuse every dream killer and bind the negative by the blood of Jesus.

Be a giant in the spirit. Tell the devil off and to go, and it shall flee. Let the Word of God break every stubborn power over your life and begin to speak life in everything you do. Let your destiny prosper in His glorious name. Ask for revival over your life and command change by faith.

I always trust Him in every situation. Even the trials that I don't understand. For example, I trust Him when I am unsure what I will eat tomorrow or how I will pay my rent. One of the great mysteries and facts about our walk with God is that we rarely understand what He's doing in our lives. If we understood, we wouldn't have any need to trust Him. I have learned to be comfortable with unanswered questions and put it in my mind that He has better and greater plans for my life.

Trust in Him—if there's something in your life you don't understand, He always makes a way.

God wants us to talk about everything. It gives Him a sense of belonging or being cared for. We should remember that we can "pray anywhere and anytime, pray always" (on every occasion read Ephesians 6:18). First Thessalonians 5:17 tells us to be "unceasing in prayer;" in other words, we need to keep the lines of communication with God open by staying in constant fellowship with Him! Many occasions before I invited the Holy Ghost in my life as my personal Savior, problems would put me in bed or get me hospitalized. Now I always give my brain a break and instead of stressing about anything. I give it all unto Him to carry it for me. That alone upsets the devil more—to see that I have faith in the Creator of All Heavens and Earth.

My God will meet all your needs in Jesus's glorious name. My journey in Christ has been wonderful so far, and a lot has happened to me. I can't share it all today, as I'm not going to finish them all if I start talking about them. I am a surprise to the many who mocked me, and I never looked back.

ESTHER
Namibia, Africa/Edmonton, Alberta

Chapter 7

The Blessings of Bible Verses

"You are of God, little children, and have overcome them, because He who is in you is greater than he who is in the world" (1 John 4:4 NKJV).

I was taught this verse at a very young age, and it has been with me ever since. Such reassuring and comforting words! No matter what life throws at us, greater is He, and He will help us overcome.

As a child, I would repeat this verse to myself whenever I was afraid of something, and it always comforted me just knowing that I was not alone in whatever I faced. As I got older, this verse was still in the back of my mind—almost like a gentle reminder that greater is He, and I was not alone.

As an adult, this is still one of my favorite passages, and I sing it to my children often, so they can store the comforting words with them always and remember that no matter how situations of life feel or how things may seem, our Lord is always with us and has overcome! Everything in this world is fleeting and will not last. Only our souls and what Jesus has done for us on the cross will last—He has overcome!

Note: I have studied this verse a little more in depth as an adult and have learned more about the real meaning behind it. I now know that it is directed toward not believing in false spirits. But it is very hard to shake the meaning my childhood self-had given the passage, and I still think of it as a sign that He is always with us.

CHANTEL
Fort St. John, British Columbia

God has brought me over some mountains. The loss of my brother to suicide, my struggle with depression and anxiety, and the passing of my parents due to cancer. My oldest brother and his wife also had battles with cancer and are doing fine now. God has brought me through it all, even though I have been struggling with an eye condition. By understanding that God is in control of every situation we face, I know He will help us through it if we learn to lean on Him. He has blessed me with a beautiful family of my own. Marriage and motherhood were both things I was afraid of, but I overcame this fear. My favorite verses are the following: "For God has not given us the spirit of fear; but of power, and love, and of a sound mind" (2 Timothy 1:7 KJV) and "I can do all things through Christ which strengthens me" (Philippians 4:13 KJV). Trust in Jesus.

PENNY
Fort St. James British Columbia

I grew up in a small town in Wisconsin. My father was serving in World War II when I was born. My mother and I lived with her parents until the war ended. I was loved as the proverbial apple of my grandparents' eyes. They were immigrants from the Netherlands—hardworking and most importantly people of deep faith. I never remember a Sunday without church worship services and Sunday school attendance. As I became older, there were catechism classes, youth meetings, Vacation Bible School (VBS), and the fun of summer church camp.

An early introduction to learning about our Lord and Savior, studying God's Word, and prayer and memorization of Bible passages have served me in numerous ways all my life. During my elementary years, I memorized Bible verses by using the alphabet. Thus, I'm still able to recall many of those Bible *A*, *B*, and *C* verses well into my retirement years. I won't share all the *A–Z* verses, but an example that I have drawn on often is the letter *C*: "Create in me a clean [pure] heart, O God, and renew a steadfast spirit within me" (Psalm 51:10 NKJV). These ABC's are my heart's hidden treasures.

BEV
Sheboygan, Wisconsin

When my dad passed away many years ago, my mom gave me one of his bibles. I have picked a few of the verses that he had highlighted.

> "My sheep hear my voice, and I know them, and they follow me: and I give unto them eternal life." (John 10:27-28 KJV)

> "But the mercy of the Lord is from everlasting to everlasting upon them that fear him, and his righteousness unto children's children". (Psalm 103:17 KJV)

WANDA
Edmonton, Alberta

Chapter 8

Belonging

It was a simple walk on a cold windy day to take a break and stretch my legs. I had been in a cancer clinic with my lovely wife. She was walking down a path that balanced quality of life with attempting to keep a degenerative disease from overtaking her. Sometimes it seemed like a lonely walk. Sometimes she asked me, "What will you do if you are alone?" Sometimes she felt alone but was not. She knew she was not alone.

We flirted with death more than some. Threatened life often brings a reality for many people because it's those times that often prove whether a person is ultimately alone or not.

During the same walk, I passed a large pond. One white swan was on the water. For years there were two, but an animal killed the swan's mate. This one was alone. A half a mile later, I saw another pond with one lone red leaf on the water. The contrast struck me, and I remembered the lone swan on the water. Am I alone in my trials? Is my wife? Are you alone in yours?

The God of the Bible displays in scene after scene that His desire is to know each human being who wants Him. Jesus talked to the disciples and said, "I will not leave you as orphans." In other words, believers will not be left alone or without a sense of belonging. John 14:18–21 is a plain-speaking statement that God does not leave a person alone if there is a call from the heart to know and believe in Jesus Christ. God is so radical about what happens that He says He will love us and show Himself to the one who is His disciple.

A relationship with Him does not guarantee that the heartaches in this broken world will evaporate, but it does mean that believers will never be left as orphans. And, when this life on earth ends, though we die, we will live with Him. That is radical.

That is my God—the one who made the universe and knows the place and circumstance of each human heart. It is not an exaggeration to state that His desire is that He wants none, not one, to perish. But, we do have a part: to believe and to call upon Him. This begins an eternal belonging that begins with Him and goes deep, affects relationships, changes lives, and never stops for those who follow Him.

ROLAND
Crozet, Virginia

I am from Britain and came to Canada when I was young, so most people assume I'm Canadian. When I got married and had children, I got the idea that I had to put aside my culture.

Fast forward to when our children started having children. My British cousin, who lives in France, came for a visit and told me about a worship conference in Wales that I needed to attend, because it was part of our legacy; our grandfather pastored for years in a village that was changed by the Welsh Revival of 1904, and it affected life for decades afterward. I had heard the conversations as a child.

It seemed like a good idea, and I wanted to go, but it was not until out-of-town friends visited and we showed them the website that it became a yes to go. They were so excited and said they would help us with costs, so the four of us went.

I love Britain and consider it home, but the trip was more than a nostalgic visit. I tell people that God kept stabbing me in the heart as He stirred up my love, calling, and passion for the nations, including Wales. I didn't understand how it would work out, but I told God I would come back to Wales. Two years later, my husband and I volunteered at the organization that sponsored the original ten years of worship, and the old building we operated in was where my other grandfather got saved!

We had to come home because a job opportunity came unexpectedly in Canada, which is good, because we ran out of money in Britain! I await further instruction in a situation I know is not yet over, but God knows the end from the beginning, and He will reveal all in His time.

God uses everything about you; He doesn't slice and dice to create a pretty picture of you that isn't the real version of who you truly are.

LOUISE
Fort St. John, British Columbia

CHAPTER 9

Forgiveness

I GREW UP in a Christian family. We were going to a church, and my parents had leadership positions in the church. One day my mom went for a ladies meeting at the church, and she came back home crying and was so upset. My siblings and I asked her what was wrong. We were so confused because we had never seen our mom crying. She was not the kind of person who would share whatever was happening in the church, and she had never shared with us whatever they had discussed. That day she told us what happened. When they were in the meeting, this lady was saying bad things about her. It was too much, and she couldn't hold herself, so she just cried there. When she told us that, my brother and I didn't take it well. I was upset and hurt, because I knew this lady very well. I never thought the lady would say that. My brother was telling my mom, "You know what, Mom? Don't worry. Don't cry. I will gang up with my friends. I know what I'm going to do to that lady."

My mom told him, "No, you don't have to do that. It's OK."

My brother and I were hurt. I told my mom, "When I see her from afar, I will change my route. I don't want to meet her—even if I see her at church, I won't greet her. How can she say that? How can she keep on hurting you when she could see you crying already?"

Years went by. I got married and was staying in another part of my country. One day I visited home, and when I got there, I was surprised to see that lady in our house talking with my mom, and they were so happy and laughing. She even greeted me well and was so happy to see me. When she left, I asked my mom why this lady was visiting her, and mentioned the fact that she greeted me so well. I reminded her of what she had done years ago. I asked how she could be so happy and talk to her like that. My mom said that she had forgotten all about that. She asked me if I was still holding on to what happened years back and said that she had forgiven her years ago. My mom said that I should learn to forgive the lady. My mom was so sorry she had talked about the situation with us and she didn't know that I had taken it that way. She was feeling guilty.

I forgave that lady. I had been really hurt and was holding on to the pain. When the lady saw me, I don't think she even knew that I had something against her. She was so happy, and my mom had forgotten about it and had forgiven her. But it was still inside me. I have learned something through this. Sometimes we don't forgive other people, and those people don't even know about it, and it disturbs us. We should learn to forgive. I've learned that when we have kids in our family, we should try not to discuss whatever grudges we have with other people because it affects them later in life. By the time you forgive those people, it's difficult to go back to your kids again and tell them why you have forgiven those people, and they should also forgive them.

It's not easy. I've learned not to share with my kids some of the things that I know will hurt them, as these things will create grudges between them and whoever has wronged me. I have learned that even when someone has wronged me, I try not to tell my kids because I don't know how it will impact their lives. That has really helped me so much. If you look in the Bible in Luke 23:34, when Jesus was on the cross, those were his last words. He said, "Father, forgive them for they do not know what they are doing."

Back home in my country, people really value the last words. People say, especially when loved ones are on their death bed, that they really want to listen. They will ask, "Before he died, did he say anything? What did he say?" They really value those words. I really value those last words that Jesus said on the cross. Forgiveness is very important in my Christian life. I should learn to forgive no matter how I have been wronged. I should learn to forgive. Forgiveness has really helped me so much. Whenever I am wronged, I pray. I pray that I should not take any steps ahead before I forgive whoever has wronged me.

EDLLINE
Zimbabwe, Africa/Red Deer, Alberta

I had a turbulent relationship with my stepfather. He came into my life when I was five. He was an alcoholic, and because I was not his child, he ignored me until he could find a chance to belittle me. When I was fifteen, my mom and stepfather divorced, and I did not have many interactions with him, except when he picked up his children—my brother and sister.

I went through years of counseling because of the mental abuse. In one counseling session, when I was an adult, married, and had children, my counselor asked me to write a healing letter that did not blame but just stated the facts of what I remember of how I was treated. I did not need to send it, but I felt my stepfather needed to know what I was still dealing with. A month later, our family was to go to dinner at my cousin's. She called and cancelled because she had been in a slight fender bender, and then my brother called and invited us for dinner. As we were sitting down for dinner, the doorbell rang, and my stepfather was at the door. He and I were shocked to see each other!

Long story short, he apologized, was stone-cold sober, and said my letter really opened his eyes. I believe God arranged this meeting, as I had already chosen to forgive my stepfather. It helped my stepfather heal from what he had done, and it helped me to heal more too in seeing that I was not an unlovable child.

WENDY
Kelowna, British Columbia

My family and I have realized that living on a second chance is not an easy thing to go through. My family and I went through emotional pain that we just can't forget. Being Christians and knowing how to forgive are the reasons we still smile and collaborate with others.

In the evening of May 2004, I remember I was wearing an orange dress mixed with a white color. It was a beautiful and a normal day like any other. At 5:00 in the afternoon, was when we heard the gunshot. We thought it was normal, but it wasn't. I wish I had an idea that those sounds of the gun were going to take my older brother. I could have done something. He was my best friend—though we fought every day, the next few minutes after fighting, we would start playing again. He was the person who held my hand on the first day of school. He would make sure I was safe and stable in my own class before he went to his own.

Imagine seeing your brother dying, and you don't have a chance to bury him. As I am telling you this, I still believe that one day I will meet my brother somewhere. I will not believe that my brother is dead until I bury his bones or have evidence that will assure me that he is really dead. I wonder how life would be now with him, living in a peaceful country. I wonder what he could be saying or doing. I can imagine what we would be doing now.

After being separated from my family for three days during the civil war in Congo, I remember receiving a phone call informing me that "your parents were shot to death." I had nothing to say. I remember saying to myself that if God's plan was for me to live without any family to remember, I would go with it. I asked God for help. If He could heal me of all the pain and make me understand life without them, then I'm OK.

I remember meeting my parents in Rwanda with my three brothers. I couldn't believe that they were alive—it was like a miracle seeing them. The first thing my father told me was that my older brother and my uncle (who had just graduated from the university) had been shot to death. My uncle was like my father in my father's absence, doing all our homework and all Dad's activities.

Living here in Canada is like a miracle. Living without discrimination, waking up every morning, and meeting people with a beautiful smile on the street. I wonder how life would be with my elder brother, who died at an early age. We wonder if we will get justice and a chance to bury my elder brother and uncle in respect. I will say we live a happy life, and we know Christ. That is enough for us.

SOLANGE
Congo, Africa/ Edmonton, Alberta

"But to you who fear My name The Sun of Righteousness shall arise With healing in His wings; And you shall go out And grow fat like stall-fed calves. You shall trample the wicked, For they shall be ashes under to soles of your feet On the day that I do this," Says the LORD of hosts."(Malachi 4:1-3 NKJV).

WANDA
Edmonton, Alberta

Chapter 10

Answered Prayer

Before Mother's Day, our pastor asked us if we could share our favorite verse and a prayer that God answered. It immediately came to me that I needed to share this with my church family and say thank you to God for saving my son Cliff.

My favorite verses are, "And he said to him, 'You shall love the Lord your God with all your heart, with all your soul, and with all your mind'" (Matthew 22:37)

> And we have seen and do testify that the Father sent the Son to be the Savior of the world. Whosoever shall confess that Jesus is the Son of God, God dwells in him, and he in God. And we have known and believed the love that God hath to us. God is love; and he that dwells in love dwells in God, and God in him. Herein is our love made perfect, that we may have boldness in the day of judgment: because as He is, so are we in this world. There is no fear in love; but perfect love casts out fear: because fear hath torment. He that fears is not made perfect in love. We love Him, because He first loved us. (1 John 4:14–19)

We who are born sinners and very quickly prove we are sinners have no hope of loving God, but God declares His love to us in that He sent His own Son to die—to pay the penalty for our sins. The Lord's resurrection is proof that our sins are paid for. Yes. We love Him, because He first loved us.

I thank God for the many prayers He has answered in my life. I want to tell you of one that God answered twenty-five years ago. My son came to know Jesus as

Wanda Dawson

His savior. He did not die and go to hell. He had been concerned about salvation, but something was standing in his way. God prepared us for what was coming.

On December 26, 1991, our family and youth group went skiing at Worsley in northern Alberta. I was feeling confident skiing, so my husband and I tried a new hill. For some reason, I flew down a dip and up a hill, and then something stopped me, and down I crashed. I tore the ligament and a piece of bone off my knee. Being that this was just the beginning of the day, I sat in the lodge while they continued to ski, thinking I just had sprained my knee and that it would be better in the morning. So 1992 started with surgery on my knee and a full-leg cast. I was attending college, and the long hallways were hard to walk on crutches, so I ended up in a wheelchair. Better than the crutches, but I can't say I loved the wheelchair. On Friday, February 14, I got the cast off my leg and had a foam brace for my leg. On Sunday my leg was swelling, so I decided not to go to church, but my husband and the younger two boys went. The older two boys, Dart and Cliff, were traveling with the basketball team. It was my oldest son's seventeenth birthday, so I was preparing a turkey supper. I put the turkey in the oven, and the Lord brought a memory to my mind of Cliff handing a white flag to his grandfather in a play at school. The white flag was a symbol of surrendering your life to Christ. Neither Cliff nor his grandfather were born again. At that point, I sat down and cried for salvation for both. I was not a crying person, so this was very unusual for me. I then sat and read Colossians, and God was so close to me. The phone rang.

The message was that Cliff has been in an accident, and he cannot feel his feet. The ambulance is coming to take Cliff and Paul back to Edmonton. The other boys are OK and at the Spruce Grove hospital.

I cried to God, "Please, Cliff cannot die. He does not know You. Please save him." Cliff was fifteen years old and loved to play basketball and be with his team. He and Dart, his older brother, had traveled to Edmonton to play in a basketball tournament. The team was traveling from Edmonton and had stopped in Spruce Grove at a gas station. Cliff and Dart flipped a coin to see who would be traveling in which vehicle. Cliff won and got into the Suburban. Unknown to us, they had taken the back seat out of it and put a foamy down, as usually someone wanted to sleep. Cliff and two other students chose the foamy on the floor.

It was snowing on the way home. A grain truck from Saskatchewan was coming along Highway 16X and converged onto Highway 16 coming out of Edmonton. The team had a convoy of three vehicles, and they were in front of the grain truck. The truck was speeding and hit the third vehicle, and it went into the ditch with six people from the school. Praise God no one was hurt, but they were very shaken. Then the truck went out of control and rear-ended the Suburban that Cliff was in, and in turn it hit an unknown car in front of it, buckling its frame. Dart was in the first vehicle, and they drove on toward home and did not know of the accident until they reached Whitecourt. Yes, this was before cell phones. Of course, I did not know all that was happening but learned these things later.

Second phone call. Cliff just accepted the Lord. I was happy and relieved, and the Lord assured me that it was better that Cliff would run in heaven, so it was OK if he didn't walk on earth, but my prayer then was, "Lord, give him his hands." The Lord did give him his hands, but his spinal cord was severed. If the swelling had gone up the cord, he would have lost his hands. He did not walk again.

At the accident, Cliff tried to find his legs but could not feel them, and his stomach was burning. He talked to an adult who was with them and said, "I am going to die, and I am going to be in hell." She said that he didn't need to go to hell but that he needed to ask Jesus to save him. Clifford, still lying in the Suburban, asked the Lord to save him and to forgive him.

When we arrived at the university hospital in Edmonton at 1:00 a.m., Cliff's face was shining, and he said, "Do not worry about me; I am saved, and I still have my hands." In telling us later how he was saved, Cliff said that before the accident, a black spirit had come to him and told him he was going to be the Antichrist. We had been studying about the Lord's coming in the youth group, so the coming of the Lord was fresh in his mind. The next day at the Christian school, Cliff was going to talk with the pastor, and the spirit appeared to him again and convinced him that if he told anyone, then the Lord would come, and his future would be sealed as the Antichrist. Clifford did not want this but did not know what to do. Satan was lying to him. What lies do we believe?

But on that day when our lives changed, Cliff lost the use of his legs, but he became a child of God. He did not struggle with bitterness, and today he is thankful to be in the wheelchair as a new person who loves the Lord. Christians from the school and from all around the world were praying for the boys. I believe this is what helped their attitudes and kept us all strong. In the third week, after being fitted with a body brace, Cliff was sitting up in the wheelchair and moving around the halls at the hospital. I could thank God for the wheelchair.

I was a little sore that they had taken out the seat and allowed the kids to be on the floor of the Suburban, but when they reconstructed the accident, they believed that if the kids had been sitting on the seat, the three of them would have died or had very severe brain damage. I am glad that I never ranted and raved about the seat being taken out, but I had to change my attitude and thank God that they had taken the seat out and that Cliff was alive. The driver's son was paralyzed, but the other student was OK. I stayed with Clifford and the driver's son in Edmonton for four months. One month at the university hospital and three months at Glen Rose Rehabilitation while the families drove back and forth on the weekends. Friends helped to renovate the house, and a stair lift was installed, so Cliff could come home.

I thank God that Cliff is saved and that he can use his hands to help others. Cliff has married, raised a child, and has stayed active in church and at Bible camp. Now he volunteers as a coach of a wheelchair rugby team. I would like to encourage mothers and fathers to pray for your children and tell them the way of salvation repeatedly so no matter what happens, they will be saved and not be deceived. Pray with them and keep communication open as to their feelings and build their faith. I encourage you to attend a church regularly so your children will know and accept that on Sundays they will be in church. Cliff was fifteen and not saved, but he never asked to stay home, as his friends were at church and a pattern had been set for him to realize it was expected of him. Hard times will come, but keep breathing and trust God. God loves your kids more than you do. Life as a Christian is the most fulfilling life you can have. Christ walks with us through it all. We have love, joy, and peace in Him. It has been twenty-five years now since Clifford walked, but if you meet him, he will have a big smile for you and a twinkle in his eyes. "I have no greater joy than to hear that my children walk in truth." (3 John 1:4, KJV).

LOIS
Dawson Creek, British Columbia

My verse is, "Oh Lord my God I cried unto you and thou hath healed me." (Psalm 30:2). I did this during my chemo treatment, and God did heal me. I prayed it when my son, Jeff, had his cancer last year, but he said he wouldn't take chemo because he saw what I went through. He said he was going to let God have His way and he suffered five months, and then the Lord took him home April 23, 2016. People called him the "Lowe's Preacher". He was a carpenter and purchased his building materials from Lowe's. Jeff would tell them about Jesus there and everywhere he had the opportunity. He really loved the Lord.

The treasure is, God is the healer. Sometimes He heals, and sometimes he doesn't, as in my son. It was his time to go to heaven. His son, David, got married in May. At the end of the wedding, a tornado came. It was just like at Jeff's funeral—during his funeral, a tornado came, and we all had to move to another room until the tornado ended. I thought it was a great coincidence. It was just like Jeff was at the wedding, and I thought about him immediately. We got a little wet from the rain, but it was a beautiful wedding. The Lord and my son, Jeff, were there.

JENNENE
Prescott, Arizona

One evening while we were pastoring in Consort, Alberta, we were driving home on a dark and stormy evening when our car lights stopped working properly. We prayed for the Lord's protection while we kept driving toward home. All the rest of the way home, every time the car lights went out, there was prolonged sheet lightning, so we could see the road, the curves, and the hills. We made it home safely. Praise the Lord!

KEN AND MYRNA
Prince George, British Columbia

Chapter 11

God is So Good

I WAS GOING through a divorce. I knew I wasn't going to stay in this town, where everybody knows your business. I had to find a good job, like, yesterday. The resource center was very helpful and supportive. I sent out so many resumes to companies every day. I was getting more worried each day that went by. Then one day I was in the living room, and the phone rang. I have never looked back. I had a phone interview and was offered the job immediately. I was working on base with the military at the time and needed to give two weeks' notice.

Talk about God's timing. I am so blessed. I prayed about having help with my move to Edmonton. People I knew as casual acquaintances—my bank manager and her husband and son—were there to help me pack a twenty-six-foot rental truck. The lady whose husband had built our house was even there to support me. And the bank manager's husband even drove the huge truck to Edmonton. I was so relieved. It was like a huge weight was lifted from me. My two bosses were very understanding, supportive, and were there for me.

The best gift I ever got was my freedom. When you are in it, you cannot see how ugly and tense the situation really is.

CAROL
Edmonton, Alberta

This happened many years ago and is not something I will forget. I was living in a house downtown. The house had a lovely front porch, and the yard was fenced. The fence had a front gate located right next to the sidewalk. My car was parked in front of my house beside a huge, beautiful maple tree. Late one night I heard a ruckus outside; I got up to check out the disturbance. I looked out the window and discovered two racoons were digging through the garbage bags I had put out that evening, and a neighbor's cat was sitting a few steps away, watching the raccoons. My first thought was how to get rid of these animals, since raccoons can get quite vicious, and I wasn't sure if they would attack if I yelled out at them. Then the thought came: rebuke them in Jesus's name. So I whispered through the window, "Leave in Jesus's name." The cat left and sat on the sidewalk, and then I said again: "Leave in Jesus's name," and the two raccoons joined the cat on the sidewalk. Well, this was not good enough, because I didn't want them to return after I went to bed. So I said, "This is not good enough; leave in Jesus's name." The raccoons walked to the end of the block, which is just a couple of doors down from my place, and hung around while the cat disappeared. I again said, "This is not good enough; leave in Jesus's name." Then a third raccoon slid down from the maple tree, and all three left. It was so amazing to experience this, but the most amazing and awesome thing that I learned was just how powerful the name of Jesus Christ is. I just had to whisper His name, and a miracle happened. There is much power in His name!

MARCE
Grand Forks, British Columbia

A treasure God has given me that has helped so much is, I love God when things are good, and I love God when things are bad. I try to keep the same intensity, and it's been a treasure of victory for me. I love God passionately when things are good, and I love God passionately when things are bad. It helps me to stay in a stable state of victory. So when it looks like God doesn't show up to answer, you just remember that it isn't important so much what God does for you, it's for who you are in Him and what He's done for you on the cross. So if God didn't do anything else for me other than dying on the cross, the cross was enough—everything else is a bonus.

BRICE
Sedro Wooley, Washington

※

In 1998, we had been living in the beautiful Okanagan city of Vernon for about a year. Although we had a wonderful church and were making some good friends, it never really felt like home. I had nothing to complain about and couldn't say why I felt so unsettled there, but I felt that it was not the right place for us. We returned to our former home city of Edmonton for a wedding. In the fall, my husband was offered a job, so we were happy to move back. Less than a year later, my husband was diagnosed with cancer. It was a very difficult time physically and emotionally. However, we were so thankful to be in a city with all of the best treatment. My husband had surgery to remove the growth and later had chemotherapy. If he had needed this type of treatment while we lived in Vernon, he would have had to travel to Vancouver. I can't imagine how I would have looked after our two-year-old daughter and nine-year-old son while he was going through that. Being in Edmonton, we were close to family that helped immensely with watching the children and so much more. And we could all be home together while he recovered and went through treatment.

Now I understand why we were so uncomfortable in Vernon, and I am so thankful God brought us here when He did. I am thankful for good doctors and medicine. And I am thankful for the support of families as well.

Satan meant to tear us down but only made us stronger. And the experience helped us to understand that God cares about us, and we can trust Him. God had His hand on us through it all!

JEANINE
Edmonton, Alberta

※

CHAPTER 12

Jesus Christ, My Redeemer

I GOT PREGNANT with my second baby in 2014, and I started seeing a change in me. Things that I liked just died (especially alcohol). I was thinking that this is just pregnancy hormones taking over. The time came when I had to name my daughter, and I asked my father, who knows more about God's things, to give me a name that speaks of God. He gave me Rijandjee (submit to God), and I used that name for my daughter. After giving birth, I tried alcohol again, and the same thing happened—there was no taste of how it was before! I started praying earnestly. God touched my heart and transformed it as I was seeking Him through a prophetic television channel. My life changed completely, and I did not hesitate to give my life back to the one who created it. After giving my life to Christ, God gave me reassuring scriptures saying He is with me and looking out for me.

John 14:26 (AMP) "But the Comforter (Counselor, Helper, Intercessor, Advocate, Strengthener, Standby), the Holy Spirit, Whom the Father will send in My name [in My place, to represent Me and act on My behalf]. He will teach you all things. And He will cause you to recall (will remind you of, bring to your remembrance) everything I have told you.

The Lord is good, and I want to encourage someone that the Lord just waits for your "yes" to the calling, and all will be well with you. All glory to God!

HINDUNDU
Namibia, Africa/Edmonton, Alberta

I would like to share my testimony of my encounter with the Lord. I want to give you readers an idea of what my character was. When the spirit of alcohol entered my body, it changed and destroyed everything about my character.

God made and blessed my soul with fullness of joy, happiness, gladness, and humbleness. Every day was a happy day for me, and I would always put a shining smile on my face. Even in times of sadness or sorrow, and even though I grew up in a poor environment, I would always put on that smile, because my Lord set me apart. And because the Lord set me apart, He made sure that His Word (Bible) was going to abide in me at a very young age, so that the spirit of God could be with me all the days of my life. I accepted the Word and the works of God in my life, and I started to walk with the Lord. God started to bless me. Even though I faced a lot of challenges in my life, God always took time to listen to my prayers and answer them. I always got what I wanted or what I didn't deserve in my life because the Lord was always making a way for me—always.

We all fall short of the glory of God if our lives are not filled with the Holy Spirit. I made one mistake in my life that changed my character. I was reading the Bible to know it or to have a knowledge about it, but I did not read the Bible to understand it and practice what I read. The devil, because he was so jealous of me, used this opportunity and brought alcohol into my life. I became in love with and devoted to alcohol—so much so that I forgot about the Word of God. The spirit of alcohol became the ruler of my mind and my life. I came to a point where I didn't want to do anything with God. I only went before God in times of need, and if things were difficult in my life, I rejected and dishonored the Lord my God. God also has a limit in our lives. If we refuse to walk with God, God will grant us our wish and depart from our lives. When God departs, the devil will take over, and we start to lean on our own understanding and think that we can be on our own and face the challenges of this world. We will then suffer big consequences, because we cannot fight the principality of darkness with our flesh, and that is why we need the presence of God in our lives to protect us.

I became the complete opposite of the person I was before. When I started to drink alcohol, I developed fear, depression, anger, and sadness in my life. If things were not going my way, I would drink as much alcohol as I could, and when drunk I would pour or dump my troubles on other people. I became a disgrace and a rejected person among whoever I came across when I was drunk.

Pride took over my life, and I let my mind believe that I was always doing the right things when I was under the influence of alcohol.

In all truth, I never found happiness when I was under the influence of alcohol. I pretended that I was happy. God can leave or depart our lives, but He never forgets about us. So I came to a point where I wanted to return to my old character, so that I could live happily with other people. I realized that what I was doing was wrong, and I also figured out that alcohol was the architect of all my problems.

I was left with no option but to quit alcohol and seek the presence of God in my life again. I gave my life to God, and I accepted Jesus Christ as my personal savior, and the Holy Spirit started to work transformations within my life. Today I read the Bible to understand, and to practice, follow, and be obedient toward the Word and the works of Jesus Christ. The truth has set me free indeed, and my old character is coming together in my life, and I am finding joy, peace, and happiness in the presence of God.

My hope and prayer is that I will remain in the presence of God forever and ever, Amen.

NELSON
Namibia, Africa/Edmonton, Alberta

"And we know that all things work together for good to them that love God, to those who are the called according to His purpose". (Romans 8:28 NKJV)

IAN
Philippines/Edmonton, Alberta

There were seven of us growing up, including my mother and father. Of the seven, we had one boy. So because of African mentality, our father did not want the girls to go to school. He only wanted the boys to go to school.

Women only got married and left the house to go work for the husbands. I don't know if he was jealous, or if he was stupid. We would go to school once in a while, but it was not enough. My heart was burning to learn. We were living in town, and our mother was a housewife. She was also a tailor and would sew dresses and trousers for people. She worked hard for us to survive. My father was a drunk, and he was drinking a lot. My two sisters and I struggled. My two younger sisters received education because our mother did what she could and our uncle helped her. The Holy Spirit came and said that He would teach me Himself. For example, the word "Bible;" I did not know what the letters said, so the Holy Spirit would say the word "Bible." When He taught me to read, He started with the Bible. I am talking about somebody who I could not see, but sometimes I could feel Him. It was somebody who I did not know, but His words come to my mind: "Do this" and "Go this way" until I could speak, read, and write. The Holy Spirit was my teacher.

One day I had a dream that I was in Canada. I was in the midst of white people. At the time in Africa, my people loved white people—wanted to be with them and would want to be among them. People would say that I was very likable. I shared this dream with my friend, and she told me that only people who have been to university can go to Canada. I didn't know God at that time. I didn't even realize the person who had taught me to read was the Holy Spirit.

When the radio was on, and I would hear news concerning Canada, my heart would jump. Why? I do not know. Around 1989, the dream began to come back more seriously. One lady came to me and said that she knows someone who is sending people to Canada. When I went to this person, he told me he could see that Canada would be good for me. "Canada is yours," he said.

One day someone called me and said, "You can go to Canada. When I was ready to come to Canada, I had a dream that I was in the middle of a street. Poor people were on the street, and some were sleeping. I woke up and said, "No, that is not Canada! Canada is a good country, and those people are poor. How can they be on the street? Not me—that is not where I'm going." I do not know if God was showing me this to help those people, to pray for those people, or if life was like this in Canada. The dreams kept coming.

One day I tried to leave to go to Canada with another lady. We flew from Africa to Dubai. We were sent back. The lady tried again, but she did not want to

49

go with me. She said that I was bad luck and wanted to go by herself. They sent her back. I tried to go to Canada again via Africa to London and was sent back. My sister said that "no matter what, you are going."

I said, "No, it is enough now. I am done with Canada."

I had a professor who told me, "God is your Father. Now I am going to pray and fast for you for seven days. I will seek God on your behalf. If they send you back, I will pay for everything. God is your daddy. You are going to go. Now you are going to go by fire!"

During the other departure times, I did not pray. When they prayed for me, I came in through Toronto—Botswana to Kenya to Amsterdam to Toronto. I didn't have any problems! The person who was doing the papers for me wrote a few things down and gave me the paper, and then made notes that I was to be taken to the Red Cross and get a stamp there.

On the second day, everything was done, and I waited for my hearing. I went to the hearing, and it took just fifteen minutes with the judge. I was having a very bad headache, and the doctor wrote a letter for me and said, "When you get back to Toronto, give your lawyer this letter." The letter said, "Don't question this person much—she has a very bad headache." The lawyer gave the letter to the judge, and the lawyer said to me that I was going to lose this case. I said to the lawyer, "The God that brought me here is somehow going to speak on my behalf. I do not want you to speak on my behalf. Just sit there and keep quiet. My God will do the rest." The judge told me to look right in his face. Many people say that the judge will ask you what the paper says, because a lot of people lie, and the document doesn't match their words. The case was finished, and I could continue my journey. I remember at one point telling God that I didn't know how to speak in the courtroom. In my dream, He said, "I am already there." Well, He was and still is with me. I praise God!

DINAH
Botswana, Africa/Edmonton, Alberta

CHAPTER 13

The Power of Blessing and Our Words

THE FIRST ACT of God upon the first people on earth was a spoken blessing. "Then God blessed them and God said to them, 'be fruitful and multiply; fill the earth and subdue it; have dominion over the fish of the sea, over the birds of the air, and over every living thing that moves on the earth'" (Gen. 1:28 NKJV).

My husband had never been blessed by his father. Instead, he had been cursed with words like, "You'll never amount to anything." He constantly sought the approval of his father to no avail. His father had been cursed as well by his dad and so could not bless his own son. Things changed when my husband received a blessing prayed over him by a spiritual father—from "Heavenly Father." He gained a confidence in his own character, a confirmation of his life calling, and a lifting of the emotional weight upon his soul.

Words of blessing carry the weight and authority of heaven. They transmit life and hope and change the way we think about ourselves. A blessing reveals heaven's perspective on who we are and where we are meant to go in life. We call that identity and destiny.

God had commissioned His people to speak blessings on His behalf. This is especially true with respect to parents blessing children.

Confession: "Shalom Aleichem. Shalom be upon you. May we be blessed with safety, with rest, with prosperity, with wholeness, with completion, with fullness, with soundness, with well-being, and with peace." (John 20:19—21, OJB).

PAMELA
Grande Prairie, Alberta

About the Author

Wanda Dawson enjoys walking in nature, where she and the love of her life, Father God, fellowship and enjoy the beauty, scents, and wonder that has been created for us. Of course, the weather in Edmonton, Alberta, is not always conducive to being outside. On poor-weather days, Wanda occupies herself indoors with prophetic art (drawing and pastels), writing, playing her keyboard, crocheting, attempting new recipes, and spending time with her family and friends. Wanda is active in her church, Beam of Hope International, particularly with the children's ministry, prayer, and intercession.

She is empathetic and passionate and has a sincere calling from God. Her desire is not only to help others understand the Word of God but to help them know and understood God's love—and also to realize their full potential in Christ Jesus.

Wanda has recently gone through a major life-changing season. You can read this in her recently published book,

Mourning into Dancing:
My Journey through Separation and Divorce.

Made in the USA
Columbia, SC
11 March 2018